Map of an Onion

Map of an Onion

Kenji C. Liu

INLANDIA BOOKS
RIVERSIDE, CALIFORNIA

Map of an Onion
Copyright 2016 by Liu, Kenji C.
ISBN: 978-0-9970932-0-9
All rights reserved

No part of this book may be used or reproduced in any manner whatsoever without the prior written permission of both the publisher and the copyright owner.

Cover art: Kenji C. Liu
Author photograph: Margarita Corporan
Book design and layout: Kenji C. Liu
Typefaces: Dolly and Abadi MT

Printed and bound in the United States of America
Distributed by Ingram

Winner of the National Hillary Gravendyk Prize

Published by Inlandia Institute
Riverside, California
www.inlandiainstitute.org
First Edition

Contents

Foreword i
Introduction vii

I.

Being Born is Also a Ghost 1
Deconstruction: Papers 3
Prayer to the God of Documents 5
Search History 7
Prelude to My Mother's Emigration 9
A History of My Complexion 10
The Battle for Durham Woods 12
In Orbit Around New York City 14
Overdue Notices 16
Powering Up 18
Photo: Peach Boy in Kyoto 20
The Ocean Swallows 23
Letter to Myself I 25

II.

Hakkas, the— 29
Portrait of Father as Intersection of Multiple Sets 30
Your Father Tongue 33
Deconstruction: No Government Can Hold a Hermit Crab 34
My Dear Koxinga 35
Advice to the Liu Family 37
A Son Writes Back 38
兒子的回應 40
Migration: Like Paul Atreides 43
Deconstruction: Citizenship 45
Elegy for Kimani Gray 46
Man Poem 48

His Pronouns Twitch	51
Immigration: Slide 78	55

III.

Tree of Heaven	59
Martian Chronicles	61
Nanji no tame / for You	63
汝のため／フォー・ユー	66
The Emperor Recognizes His Children	69
Ah Kung in the Philippine Jungle, 1945	72
Golden	74
So that you are always sir, dear sir	76
Para que siempre sea el señor, estimado señor	79
Deconstruction: Capital	82
Memoriam for Places	85

IV.

Landing	89
Oboetaro / oboenakatta daro	91
Deconstruction: Pink	92
Migratory Daughter	93
Heart Sutra After Cremation	95
Native Language	96
Letter to Myself II	97
May These Words Be Worth Speech	100
How to Be an Orange	102
Between the Two	105
Deconstruction: Body Unbound	107

Notes	112
Gratitude 合掌	117
Acknowledgements	119

Foreword
A Poetry of Interruption
Timothy Yu

Birth certificates, passports, citizenship papers: these
are the documents that define our official identities, that
make us legible to the apparatus of the state. For Asian
Americans, such documents are often central to our family
narratives, marking a history of migration, departure and
arrival, rejection or belonging. Yet we are also well aware
of what such official documents erase, enforce, or repress.
Our "arrival" as Americans marked by a naturalization
certificate may be predicated upon the erasure, willed
or not, of our histories and even our names, as well as
the exclusion of others—including our own ancestors.
And no document can protect Asian Americans from
the presumption that we do not belong in a nation that
continues to equate Americanness with whiteness.

Kenji Liu's *Map of an Onion* begins with a reflection on
the role of such documents in shaping identity, evoking in
the poem "Deconstruction: Papers" the author's own birth

certificate, passport, and naturalization certificate. But the poem's subtitle—"after Theresa Hak Kyung Cha"—shows that Liu is also placing himself within a tradition of Asian American interventions into the official construction of identity. Liu's allusion is to Cha's 1982 masterwork, *Dictée*, and in particular to *Dictée*'s famous opening sections, which depict a French dictation exercise in which an overly literal pupil writes down every word spoken, including "comma" and "period." Critics have seen Cha's pupil as an exemplar both of the process of interpellation and the resistance to it; this is a subject formed in language but also resistant to it, a "bad" translator who disrupts the intended flow of ideological incorporation.

Liu extends and deepens Cha's intervention through a remarkable device: he "interrupts" the documents themselves with other languages, a move that reflects his own border-crossing history. His "birth certificate with Chinese interventions" injects his Taiwanese heritage into the record of his birth in a Japanese hospital, while the language of his naturalization certificate is interrupted by words from the Lenape language. The latter intervention reflects Liu's movement beyond a narrowly Asian American framework to incorporate a historical awareness of indigeneity and colonialism: Asian Americans' own claims to "Americanness" must themselves be understood as implicated in a history of colonization and genocide.

It is this multiethnic, coalitional sensibility that is most characteristic of Liu's highly original contribution to Asian American writing. *Map of an Onion* includes poems written in, or translated into, English, Chinese, Japanese, and Spanish; the map Liu creates in his book is necessarily a multilingual one, ranging as it does from Asian immigrants to disappeared Mexican students. Liu's work may be most insistently political in its refusal to be satisfied with the individual narrative, and in its placing of those stories in much wider social and historical contexts.

Yet Liu's work is also movingly and engagingly personal. "Even newborns have papers," he observes in the collection's opening poem, "Being Born is Also a Ghost." This collection, as Liu wryly puts it in the title of one poem, is a "Search History," but one that can't be found through Google; instead, it is driven by the search for his own parents. "I chase their bright twenties," he writes, imagining their meeting. "My eyes try to find them." The collection's multilingualism is also quite simply a reflection of the speaker's own history, a "search translated / between my family's four languages." The challenge Liu sets for himself—to capture the scope and sweep of history while "trying / not to lose / the feathered details"—is the challenge of much contemporary Asian American poetry, and indeed of political poetry more broadly.

It's striking, then, that one way Liu finds to access

this nexus of the personal and historical is through an
exploration of forms, from forms of classification to
the Chinese poetic form of the qilu. The card catalog
and the encyclopedia make featured appearances. The
father is imagined as "an intersection of multiple sets."
Found poems employ collage to reflect on ethnicity and
Marxist theory. Perhaps this interest in form is where
Liu's investigation of the ideologies of documentation
meets the poetic impulse: if the birth certificate, the
passport, and the encyclopedia reflect the structures of
official ideology, poetry may offer a counter-structure,
one in which official systems can be deconstructed
and interrupted by the system of the poem.

Liu is contemporary enough, and critically aware
enough, not to believe naively that the poet can simply
escape from oppressive systems or resist them through
inversion. "Even a baby," Liu writes in "Prayer to the
God of Documents," is "a filing system for breath." But
Liu, following predecessors like Theresa Hak Kyung Cha
and Myung Mi Kim, wonders whether we might find a
space of action in the shuttling between systems, in the
diasporic movement among nations and languages. Liu's
use of the form of the qilu, which uses an eight-line stanza
of seven syllables each, embodies in its very structure
a different kind of history, a centuries-long ancestral
tradition into which the speaker inserts himself, and to

which he presumes to speak back. The movements of the qilu are, as Liu puts it, "brief traces" drawn on "onion skin paper"—seemingly fragile and ephemeral, but surprisingly enduring in the face of the rigid ideologies of the nation.

The mapping Liu offers us in this collection rejects the sharp boundaries of the official cartographer. Instead, *Map of an Onion* is a border-crossing, coalitional text that finds its political voice in interruption. In Liu's poetics, family history structures, and is structured by, histories of migration, colonialism, and violence, yet Liu finds in the interstices of those structures a space of profoundly personal exploration. "Tell me how to say your name," he asks us, "because / documents won't protect us."

— *Timothy Yu*
    University of Wisconsin–Madison
    Author, *100 Chinese Silences*
    and *Race and the Avant-Garde: Experimental*
    and Asian American Poetry Since 1965

Introduction

Chad Sweeney

One way to read *Map of an Onion* is as a quest myth for the contemporary self—discovering, revealing, asking deeper, inquiring layer by layer toward the onion's core, which is, ironically, unlocatable. Self as sensorium of perception, self as "animal, bird," as family member, as the inheritor of eight centuries of Liu heritage, self as man, as Japanese-Chinese-Taiwanese-American living on borrowed Lenape Native land in a suburb of New Jersey, self as unstable construct, as citizen, diplomat, *flaneur*, *saboteur*, artist, as tech-savvy, code-switching trans-lingual being.

In "History of My Complexion," the poet describes himself as "a big fancy kaleidoscope . . . made in 1977" and a "flame of leaves / in autumn." By contrast, the U.S. immigration official processing this two-year-old boy's entry from Japan is unable to escape the black and white binary in reducing young Kenji to an X in a box, "elevated threat / level yellow." A central dynamic of living today is this antagonism between one's self-perception and external lenses such as those of Nation, history, language, gender, racism, religion, even family heritage, which exert pressure to define, to name, to claim. Kenji Liu's *Map of an Onion* labors to recognize (and to de-colonize) the full, prismatic Self—a self in the multiple, the all-of-these-at-once kaleidoscopic shifting Self with its "bouquet of in-betweens."

One layer of the onion maps the private experience of lived moments changing through ripples of sense perception as "leaves in autumn." One layer maps the self as a storm of molecules, one atom from Okinotorishima, one from "the whisker point of a catfish." One layer of the onion traces a genealogy of family narratives where Liu's story begins in New Jersey, or in Japan during American occupation, or in Taiwan during Japanese occupation or further back toward sources beyond reach. The lineage is a history of leaving and crossing and adjusting, which parallels the stories of nations, of exile, of disintegration and survival in resilience and hybridity, as well as the psychic migrations of the writer in his own lifetime. How a living, current self negotiates the present against all the lineages of inheritance from a past rich with contradictions. Liu's task is not to resolve these contradictions or to choose one lineage over another, but to inhabit them in the fullness of their dynamic interplay.

To achieve this the poet occupies a range of emotional
and intellectual registers, including a heartbreaking elegy
sequence for his mother which sets the Buddhist *Heart
Sutra* as pervading prayer chant, "no body, no eyes, no
ears, no mouth," in manifesting the *ultimate dimension*
through the lens of non-self and interdependent arising
against the physical decline, death, and cremation
of the body. The body *is* and *is not*—a body empty-of-
body which contains the entire universe—as "mom's
creased hands writing / dark snowflakes of kanji." The
sequence concludes with this delicate stanza:

> Write the sutra so neatly a bird reads it
> from space, so tenderly my dead touches
> her own cheek, startled.

One layer of the onion interrogates inherited ideas of
manhood, "this tired front of manhood . . . I seek its soon
destruction," manhood represented by batting cages, or
the murder of a Japanese boy trick-or-treating, or as a
monster pickup truck taking up two parking spots. Liu
seeks for new images of manhood, "thirsty for what can't
be summarized." One mapping is the male body, itself,
inherited and earned, resistant, "docile" and occupied—
property of the State and site for punishment—such
that self-mapping is an act of post-colonial sovereignty.

To reflect the plurality of this America now, Liu summons a potent range of dictions, lexicons and languages—juxtaposed, dialoguing, making competing claims on the individual, yet encouraging an expansion of consciousness, an elastic polyglot poetic. The poems include English, Japanese, Spanish, Chinese, the international phonetic alphabet and hybrid blends which both inform and destabilize, such as the Lord's Prayer in Romanized Japanese, rendering such surprising phrases as "Yeast, the great baker has landed" and "Tofu is no holy metaphor . . . Open your ports. Rise. Eat."

Beyond Liu's precise, lapidary free verse, this poetry houses the ancient Chinese *qilu*, the Deconstruction, letters to self, immigration and birth documents, the sutra chant, the photograph, the palimpsest, a film slide, found language from an outdated encyclopedia, prayer, a hospital form, an answering machine message, elegy, passport and biblical verse. Liu's agility in language may be his most remarkable achievement, that he dialogues meaningfully among so many forms and lexicons, that he gathers into our field of consciousness so much of the world's inheritance, of scripture, deconstruction and post-colonialism, of Derrida, Butler, Theresa Hak Kyung Cha and Foucault—all in the breath of lyric poetry, emotionally alert, humorous, elegiac, alive and original—that his anxieties and triumphs trace such beautiful, inclusive shapes. This feels like the fulfillment of a promise, and a new promise made.

In the poem "A Son Writes Back," Liu responds to a *qilu* written by his patriarchal ancestor who predicted eight-hundred years ago that "foreign lands will become home." Ironically, this sets the course for Liu's inheritance of migration and adaptation, to make a *home* in change, both personally and artistically, to weave a nest from instability "with a suitcase full / of dew." Ultimately, then, this map of an onion is also a *mapping* of the *onioning*, of the onion's openings and hiddenness, of the processes of revealing the liminal spaces between layers, where at the onion's core, we find, paradoxically, its surface once again.

Kenji Liu's illuminated *Map of an Onion* is a koan of deconstructions which interrogates within the fissures of difference those spaces within us and between us, as charged spaces of potential and becoming. A book-length question in a hard, graceful calligraphy, asking deeper, asking better, what does it mean to be a self, this Self, to "translate this search / between my family's four languages,"—emergent, reassembled of ancient molecules and sculpted by all the forces of culture, history and bloodlight into a man? If "nations need a parable to reinvent themselves," *Map of an Onion* may be that parable.

— *Chad Sweeney*
  Hillary Gravendyk Prize Judge

"Because it is psychotic not to know where you are in a national space."

– BHANU KAPIL

Being Born is Also a Ghost

Kyoto, Japan

Year of the snake. 4:12 pm. A forest, river, and hospital.
He looks me in the eyes. Between us, an engineer and a painter.

He steeps in his first tangerine afternoon, takes leave of ghosts.
I attend to his nascent day of migration.

A bureaucrat's pen is an axe, is a wall. Even newborns have papers.
Document in my hands. Gold foil embossed. Baby and a bowl cut.

Like the dead, he has a country—but no shoes.
I try to remember what matters. What time will his feet become mine?

Down the street, a war temple built with stolen trees.
What is the opposite of yes when no is forbidden?

His mouth opens, words jump in, then a book, then a flag.
I teach him to light a match, and search for my face in his.

Deconstruction: Papers

after Theresa Hak Kyung Cha

EXHIBIT A.
BIRTH CERTIFICATE WITH CHINESE INTERVENTION

This is to certify that Liu dòuhào Chien liánjihào Shu was
born at four bi hào twelve P jùhào M jùhào o piē hào clock
on Feb period twenty dòuhào nineteen seventy seven at The
Japan Baptist Hospital jùhào

EXHIBIT B.
TAIWANESE PASSPORT WITH ENGLISH INTERVENTION

all caps chinese consulate general end caps New York, N
period Y period comma all caps u period s period a period
end caps Seen at this Consulate General comma duly
endorsed to be good for proceeding to all caps all countries
except communist controlled countries and areas end
caps via all necessary countries en route period all caps c k
ning consul consulate general of the republic of china new
york end caps Date colon Jun fifteen nineteen seventy-six
Fee colon all caps us end caps dollar sign two underlined
superscript zero zero No period colon nine zero one
zero two

EXHIBIT C.
NATURALIZATION CERTIFICATE WITH
LENAPE INTERVENTION

Personal description of holder as of date of naturalization kènu Date of birth February twenty kènu nineteen seventy seven kènu sex Male kènu complexion Medium kènu color of eyes Black kènu color of hair Black kènu height three feet zero inches kènu Marital status Single kènu Country of former nationality Republic Of China I certify that the description above given is true kènu and that the photograph affixed hereto is a likeness of me alà

Name Changed By Decree Of The Court From
CHIEN-SHU KENJI LIU, As Part Of Naturalization.

Prayer to the God of Documents

Sakyo-Ku, Japan

Even a baby is

a paper cut theater,
a necklace of incisions strung together
into a country.

Is a filing system
for breath.

Though born of
a suitable mother,
he is a flock of trespasses,

sharp edges folding
inward from his father's
passport.

If he is worthy,
may the red ink measures
of this one-eyed world
unwrap,

hurry him from the hospital
through bloodshot evening,
away from uplifted noses of hounds.

He is rain and rust,
full of sea and its wide open,

not a flag or a reason or treason.

Let him sail across an octopus arm
and recite fish sutras in your name,
never to be a fist
or any finger in it.

Release him from all paper,
that first wound
commissioned
to condense

his unfolding life.

Search History

for my parents

>I chase their bright twenties—
>and the church steeple of their youth.

The shrine folds in—factory of small wings—

Zoom and inhale the traces of their hajimemashite
    in tides of traffic, rain, fish.

>*The route he swims—from colony to metropole,*
>*through dust of sugar and camphor.*

>On the church camping trip—he makes eyes
>at a girl—who later marries her god.

>>The night where he finally sees *her*.
>>Street view of their first stroll after Sunday mass—
>hands polite as warm summer rain.

How she comes to love him—country boy rising from the edge
    of her father's erstwhile empire, into the heart.

My eyes try to find them—columns of insistence
        scrolling through the underbrush.

            My shadow, a kaiju on their map.
            Their welcome, uncertain as yet.

    Ikimasureba, doko ni ikimasho ka?

        This search translated
        between my family's four languages—trying

        not to lose
            the feathered details
    of their tiny, hand-drawn hearts.

Prelude to My Mother's Emigration

She unwinds her spool—
        but for years she girds, weaves fog
into mountains, advances and relents.
                A violin bow.

        After war, after occupation,
the Americans make good with conveniences
                and a thimble dream.

She listens to the pacific hum beckon.
        Faint echoes in the landscape,
                thoughts wrapped in night static.

She unfurls,
        releases her coils,
        threads brightness.

        Sparks.

A History of My Complexion

or how mr. molyneux of the superior court categorized
me when i was naturalized

my two year-old bowl cut
apostrophe eyes
blue and gold sneakers

were no match for
his smoke sputtering
black and white brain.

he worked proper names,
paper cuts, fences and
right angles, a mad scientist.

at three feet zero inches
and twenty-eight pounds:
my complexion was "medium"

a half-cooked steak
or elevated threat
level yellow

but i was certain i was
a big fancy kaleidoscope
made in 1977

a flame of leaves
in autumn, a bouquet of
in-betweens.

The Battle for Durham Woods

"New Jersey Pipeline Explosion Sets Off Panic, Chaos and Fear"
THE NEW YORK TIMES, MARCH 25, 1994

In elementary school I
crouch under the desk
Memorize bomb shelter addresses

An elderly neighbor
says to my M&M fundraiser
We fought you in Japan and buys peanut

My parents and I fold
each other in pajamas and stare
up at the suburban mushroom bloom

Happy little fireball
Bob Ross chirps
Brush singeing the black sky

Ground Zero
says the governor
rushing back from Florida

We didn't know anyone
in Hiroshima or Nagasaki
my mother mentions softly

The burned apartment complex
is racially integrated
                notes *The Times*

Rescue dogs go home
Officials swarm the crater
Praise the dead

The Cold War
rumbles onward
under a single terrible eye

In Orbit Around New York City

Edison, New Jersey

Eight stops from Penn Station.
Unsuspecting universe, unzipped.
The leaning four o'clock sunlight
a warm bridge for my cheek.

Nearest river in my atlas—
an interstate that taught me
to be an on-ramp. On the mantel
a book of Chinese inventions.

A town named for the light bulb's
daddy. Circled up round a borough
bearing a Lenape chief's name.
Ghost maps are hungry maps.

Over the decades, onion skins
laid with scalpels. Tributaries,
deveined. Villages risen of dirt.
Maps stumbling from bushes.

After the farms
        the woods
        the negro colony
               the tracks
               the burning crosses
                      the factory
                      the old tavern—
                               Dublin, Sicily.
                               Mumbai, Taipei, Manila.

Every rest stop a borrowed word.
Metuchen, Manhattan, Piscataway.
Every word a buried world.
Translucence. Diffusion. Frost.

Every layer of history in a thing.
Steel cotton lungs. The tight air
even under the suburbs.
Especially under the suburbs.

Overdue Notices

1982-1994

Holy card catalogue, apothecary for the
left behind. Mornings: trains and avenues
suck commuters into the city, drain them
back for dinner and evening news.

Alone, you need. Take residence in shelves
Asimov to Zahn. Summon savage men hunted
by zeppelin women, launched from snow-globe
cities. Amazons in lamé, laser on each hip.

You know which volumes haven't yet come
home. A child's long days. Books sigh and crinkle
in the couch, host you till twilight. They
carry you tirelessly to the end of every Earth.

Suburban cold sleep. Across the deep nights
between galaxies, glue binds every possible
universe. A supernova queen waits somewhere in
her celestial city, painted by red stars.

Returning, always, to the catalogue. Querying
the drawers for new ways to fly the days.
So many light-years between child and migrating
adult. So much overdue.

Powering Up

Red LED basking in its motherboard,
        stabbing the dark with
modem calls.

Tiny campfire,
        base camp for my kilobytes.

I load starlight,
run the program.

In the next time zone, dad reads
the news in snow banks—sends
paychecks—sends brightness—
misses the event horizon.

Clouds settle in our database—though

mom's hands are feathered
        counterweights, a firm unfurling
that wraps the cosmos.

Pretty soon I'll unload into
        the round, meaty world,
my tender brain
              a blinking cursor.

Though glasses thick,
        I fit on one floppy.

I'm not some pixeled plumber
        bumping bricks for fire flowers,
but yes—some drain pipes hide
            gold coins.

Unplug—
        trigger the luminescent level.

I sit cross-legged on the floor
        and unfocus my gaze.
Just a swinging
door.

        Hello, world.

Photo: Peach Boy in Kyoto

I.

Long brush stroke of coal over left eye,
you are a raven stooped on asphalt.
Wings back, praying to the smoke between your ribs.

Sullen is favored in these years. Your mouth
is a feather trying to sweep into adulthood.

Concrete purpose still not arisen, but urgency of heart—
a small cup ready to fill with purpose.

Float a bed in the Pacific and call it home.
Circle it with coral and ennui.

Forfeit a postal address, observe the mailbox rise
and sink as moon breathes you. Impersonal as salt.

(*Trapped in a state of imaginary grace.*)

II.

Summer, framed by ojiisan's tobacco smoke.
A settling layer of cicada shells.

Aluminum foil and mixtape wings.
Extended play afternoons. Walkman pilgrimages.

You're a careful composition of magnets,
iron filings flower from your mouth.

A subtle arrangement of counterpoints. Each lung
you fill, a life preserver.

(Trapped in a state of imaginary grace.)

III.

Now you reach out and something reaches back.
You, a starfish who thinks in all directions.

Strike your tuning fork hard until your
smoke shivers. Until under the armor, you vibrate back.

The Ocean Swallows

My father shows me how
to cast a single line into the Atlantic's wet mouth.

Such small hope, to flick a filament and await
reply from disinterested flesh.

The ocean has its own siren manifesto:
salt, knuckles, hate mail from whales.

On the scalloped shore,
Algonquian syllables write into us.

(If Captain Taylor had followed Lady Liberty's
tarnished curves into the cove,
he would have seen old industrial arrogance—

coral skyscrapers dodging lancets of light
thrown up by our economies of want.
Dialectic of expansion and oil.)

After a spiral of hermit crab shells
circles our afternoon, we step into
the paper maché sun. Dine on trout.

Big blue swallows our tracks,
eyelids open, close.

(The soaked distance between disasters—
its indigo brush, big enough for everything.)

Letter to Myself I

Tell me how to say your name, because
documents won't protect us.

The hospital chopped your country off,
but you're a cute paper cut.

A pair of cranes is aflame in the marsh—
your birth certificate, a twist of ash.

I want to wrap your feet in my hands,
pull the moon down for your bath.

In New Jersey, they'll trust you with cars,
dynamite, and a rebellious spirit wisping half-empty.

But you won't fill their check boxes
with your five cent loyalty. Too many questions.

Maybe freedom is a field with a sharp fence,
no matter who gives it to you.

What did you leave at the gate?
I'll look behind you as you arrive.

When I say this is love, do you believe me?

Hakkas, the—

found poem

compared with the Jews; their caste in China;
>   their industry; their persecution in China;
>   Formosa their refuge; they become indispensable to Formosa;
> they quarrel with Fokienese; their dislike for the authorities;
>   their communities well armed and fortified; savage property
> falls into their hands;
>   a settlement of, slaughtered by General Sun; hillmen,
>   added to the Imperial forces;
>   they fight the French at Tamsui; their guns and their shooting;
> considered dangerous neighbors; beheading of;
>   enrolled as Chinese troops; rebellion raised by;
>   production of sun-dried tea by; hill manufacture of
>   camphor by;
> savage raids on; warfare with savages in camphor districts by;
>   employment on narrow-gauge railway of; authority of
>   mandarins disputed by;
>   petroleum utilized by; immigration of; Chinese
>   immigrants from Kwangtung province, known as;
>   characteristics of

Portrait of Father as Intersection of Multiple Sets

You witness the worn heels
of his calculations
        how he transforms probabilities
into butterflies

               minute feet
fluttering his spine.

They unpin themselves
divide

        decades into long
airplane trips.

        Landscape
with nuclear family as isosceles

and father as vertex—
but crux, not often.

Feral helicopter seeds
        engulf

           his perpendicular shadow
raise roundhouses from stolid earth
thread arrow slits with laser beams.

He rears his wingspan
at the great stain
       edging across the strait.

Offers you advice
not consolation.

Kneels among his equations
and digs—
           eliminates variables.

The fist he shakes
at your overflowing

                 hair.

      At the tarmacs
      that carry him
      away

        rattling the ancestral rolodex
        still calling out exodus.

Son and father as parallel lines
neither adding
        the other for years.

And yet at the graph's mid-point
a caterpillar of translation.

Tell me about the bodhisattva
carrying infinite pollen
    even for us.

Your Father Tongue

Swallowed by your childhood tongue,
your face is free and the earth less wounded.
The past opens wide, controversial no longer,
and you roar like the ocean—
bold, free of the pronouns that stumble your teeth.
When you're swallowed, the jungle closes its eyes.
In pollen dreams, papayas unfold whole
and bamboo forests kneel down like tigers.

Then you shake in your sleep as mountains return
to line your mouth with their mists—
this country called home
weighs more than the years can digest.
Your voice bends, leans in to widen the cracks:
The taste of granite dust. Your first words.

Deconstruction:
No Government Can Hold a Hermit Crab

Curl into any house. A shell is a thing
of great value, but we're stand-ins for rifle,
spy, and hammer. It's policy to record
the coordinates of our feet when we dream,
to track us past the death line.

Shipments and weather glide back and forth
while we hitchhike on fickle fiscal angels.
Scuff our knees for brute sacrament.
Our country is a church inside a bank.
Dead calcium raised up into a golden ratio
of bricks and steel. If only crossing over didn't
cut in half. This: we will fold every rule
into the others, until no house can hold.

My Dear Koxinga

qilu series

1.

Your mother's a knife in the
tempest's eye. Her sleeve slices
the squall in halves, summons moss
islands. Your father's country,
razed by fists. Trailing moist and
mawkish flags, folded into
unnatural anthems, you're
a legend in therapy.

2.

You're a treaty briefer than
all its footnotes. The best seed
a state could want. Filial
and lecherous government—
three bureaucracies' worth of
wandering eyes, document
groping, teeth gripping flags like
silk underwear. Egg licking.

3.

Nations need a parable
to reinvent themselves with.
Dread breeds patriotism.
My willing antique, you're held
together with band-aids and
wind-worn nylon. Whose name is
written in the heart's passport—
are you a sovereign light?

4.

Brief traces of your passage
gilded into onion skin
paper. Your vellum quivers
under their hungry fables.
Three times your body is split.
Soldiers angle for fragments
in the strait. Lusting for the
wrong jewels, the full moon spills.

劉氏家訓

廣傳公

駿馬騎行各出疆
任從隨地立綱常
年深外境猶吾境
日久他鄉即故鄉
早晚忽忘親命語
晨昏須顧祖爐香
蒼天佑我卯金氏
二七男兒共熾昌

Advice to the Liu Family

Gong Guang-Chuan, 1250 CE

Stay on course crossing borders.
Uphold ethics where you dwell;
foreign lands will become home.
Recall your parents' teachings;
e'vry day burn fragrance to
venerate your ancestors.
Heaven bless the Liu household.
Young men, prosper together.

A Son Writes Back

qilu series

After you, we crossed many
borders. Eight hundred suns turned.
After you, a pegasus
landed two boys in Taiwan.
Mā/mǎ carried babies but
boys carried our name, the first
compass. This bypass is our
family, is our paddle.

We live with barbarians
who know not what they do. But
the three principles twist us
from sand grains into boulders.
We crease and knot, compress and
fold. A flower pressed inside
an encyclopedia
still doesn't learn anything.

Eighteen Liu generations
exit mountains of Taiwan
enter malls of New Jersey.
My papers state "medium"

complexion, the threat level
to their city on a hill.
Our nest rests uneasily,
chainsaw on an empty branch.

Beautiful blues guitar place
you hold our first bold ashes
with salt-sodden lilac seas,
steel-ribbed paper palaces,
lulling my man heart to break.
You set my rimed house adrift
in the tides repeatedly
weeping like hands in old silk.

The tired front of manhood,
motley and unforgiving.
I seek its soon destruction.
We'll make a new heaven from
long miles of broken fences,
humble pigeon feathers, and
afternoon light in a jar.
A hundred lifetimes, ending.

兒子的回應

自您之後八百日
咱越過疆土無數
自您之後一飛馬
載兩男孩來台住
婦女留家育兒女
唯有男孩傳族名
婦女無名但仍是
家族和驅動槳柱

我們與異族為伍
異族昧知己所為
三個原則把我們
從沙粒變成巨石
咱異鄉人勞筋骨
苦心志沒了自我
如花瓣壓扁書裡
未能尋取黃金屋

十八代劉氏家族
離開多山的台灣
來到繁華的新州
我膚色被列中暗

上　在　高　高　對　為　成
脅　恐　的　府　政　地　當
安　不　空　中　家　們　我
榕　的　中　　　居　園　猶
　　樹　　　　　　　如

處　音　樂　調　懷　次　藍　首　麗　美
灰　捧　骨　香　丁　漬　紋　鹽　　　您
海　花　的　的　紙　似　觸　　　　　與
樓　華　心　包　我　了　家　已　　　鋼
碎　心　冰　潮　寒　置　屢　　　　　引
覆　包　裡　中　之　如　咽　　　　　我
浮　冰　　　絹　舊　　　　　　　　您
手　潮　　　中　　　　　　　　　　嗚
　　中

概　氣　子　的　倦　怠　是　我　用　失
情　無　男　紛　　　　　　　　色
　　結　又　亂　　　　　尋　綿
　　束　是　的　　　　　求　長
籬　圍　早　鴿　　　　　殘　的
羽　毛　點　子　　　　　破　　　和
光　餘　午　　　　　　　　　瓶
堂　的　後　　　　　　　　　中
幕　天　　　　　　　　　　　締　讓
　　　　新　　　　　　　　　造　百
　　　　生　　　　　　　　　　　世
　　　　落　　　　　　　　　　　人
　　　　　　　　　　　　　　　　來

Translation:
Der-Jin Woan
and Suh-Ling Lin

Migration: Like Paul Atreides

I.

—forced into red desert from
a world of beloved oceans—the dreams slipping through
my nights owe their tides to the bottomless.

Mind touches one possibility of place,
then another, and builds a bridge of light between.
The heaviness of my cage crossfades, luminous.

In the iris fold, I consider what it means to be
locatable. Seventy percent of my molecules are hydrogens
and oxygens, the fingernails of stars.

Then atoms: At least one from Okinotorishima,
and its neighbor from the whisker point of a catfish.
The rest are the sighs of everyone who leaves.

Scent of spice in my hair. Dark anise. Marjoram, dulcet kare.
I need their fragrant spin, their underground currents
and crescent pools. And singular traces in my deepest dust.

II.

The emperor descends in night vision goggles.
Motions forward hardened soldiers and policies twisted
into bullets. Cue old world glam rock and eye shadow.

Sting smirks behind a golden blade, his pretty, heaving chest
a fence they patrol all night. But we have megaphones. We have
the power of renaming. And the shadow of rain in the orchard.

Underneath the longitude and latitude of our battles,
a vast network of caves, wet from collecting us. The darkness
contemplates from below as I step across. Thump. Thump.

Deconstruction: Citizenship

HAVE YOU EVER BEEN A MEMBER OF OR IN ANY WAY ASSOCIATED EITHER DIRECTLY OR INDIRECTLY WITH?

Indirectly a biometric hazard, activate. Associated with a cold rubber stamp. Are we within earshot of a dissection table? Your eagle describes each tremor of the splay. Country and body at right angles. A constant misspelling of membership.

HAVE YOU EVER ADVOCATED EITHER DIRECTLY OR INDIRECTLY THE OVERTHROW?

Flag, a grip of directions.

Cardboard crosses the border, bristling with folds.

How the capitol slaps heaven with its ambition.

My mother, who never became one of you, who filled her stomach with electricity. Couldn't overthrow the surgery of documents.

Are you my republic of paper?

Elegy for Kimani Gray

16 years old

Sharp tenure of boots in this callow country
    grown from open skulls. A raw harvest of bullet casings

arranged in a perfect ring around you,
    a ruthless departure gate from your too-short life.

Old bricks laid on mud, on ancient bones.
    A crooked wall that slithers in all directions, into all of us.

In the subway station, your hymnal of hail,
    audible through the sagging window pane, and

the hushed light of a penny keeping to itself,
    away from the wicked maledictions of trigger fingers.

This ending is the middle, halfway between genesis
    and the great throwing open of all our secretive vaults.

Bullet one, entitled to flesh and the sin of pride.
    Two more in thrall to the scent of a black body. With orders

from their gods, they plow your emptied land.
    Still more, cloaked against simple pleas of muscle and bone.

The last bullet, addicted to death's sharp edges,
    cracks your final seal. Your murder, a cage we have seen before.

No more. Hold every lucid moment close, so that
    its delicate turbulence does not escape your accounting.

Those who have mispledged to protect will never
    own this moment. It is yours alone, whether they pierce

mesh with metal or lies. You are not theirs,
    only yours alone. Your bright eyes open again and again,

fireflies in their factory of dark rituals. Traveling
    the undiscovered country, you are : finally : every last breath.

Man Poem

Let's fold maps so our places can meet—
my muscles have been everywhere.

I should be at the batting cages.
I should be cheering for America.

I point at home and ride the other way.
I should drink more cheap beer.

*A docile body is one that may be subjected,
used, transformed, and improved.*

Real men win with knowing looks,
with killer strut.

I like them. I like to be them.

Between these four corners
there's a catwalk. I show off my moves.

Up and down a graveyard
of cheerleaders.

I can fill every athletic cup
with my cowboy theme park.

Bricks and knuckles.
Sand and eyelids.

*This docile body can only be achieved
through strict regiment of disciplinary acts.*

These are battlefields I have built.
Do you like what I've done with my craters?

Department of Homeland Security
likes them. Wants to be in them.

I should be grilling chicken sausages.
I should be wiggling my pecs.

Oh Hummer, let's find
a Smart car to flip.

Let's watch the game so I can
blow my new volcano.

Ashes and lungs.
Sawdust and long, long tongues.

His Pronouns Twitch

with lines from Judith Butler

Let the son be a son, father be a father,
minister be a minister, ruler be a ruler.
—KONG FUZI

I. ta

Under the armor, a metal fleck.
Bounding, forming, deforming.

Asleep in the shape
of a golden bean.

A warm animal.
A twitch of night.

Below the breath of meat
hundreds of quiet names.

II. ta (他)

His name is massaged
into the regime.

Without question!
In his hand, a new passport.

Confirmation
is a body.

Forcibly materialized
his output increases.

Light cooperates with the king
and becomes the record.

The empire looks wonderful
from here. The emergency
closes.

III. ta (她)

Shame is an aspect of creation.
Demarcate, circulate, differentiate.

In the family shrine
a doorway flickers, swallows her.

Forcibly materialized
her output increases.

Perhaps to flee
would be a stronger position, but

she is also
ursus, flamecrest, emerald.

IV.

Let the very few virtuous remaining
remove the hook, and unfollow.

Brightness hidden also means
brightness wounded.

The body is exactly empty
and emptiness is exactly body.

Eventual task of smoothing
the father's path from this world.

Into all rising and passing selves
fracture ta into flutter, into new rain.

What's left:
Monsoon, white undershirt, cigarettes.

The empire of men
folds its song about the body.

While this has small pleasures—
a chant of destroyed names.

Immigration: Slide 78

Stars swim across a broken
lake— fireflies scattered
into swallowing void.

In the breakages it's realer
than a knife edge's edge.

Details pop leap—
dandelions in your childhood
yard bright yellow reactions
 to rain.

 Your father
with lawn mower triple-striped cotton
socks choke the tops of his calves.

A white kid pushes yours down
and conveys your only country's
entry price.

Every house is cracked
and light sees itself in the rifts.

         Self is
                    a reaction   composed of
      smaller reactions.

      Dispositions
                 rising   into the farthest sky
                        and then,
                                        gone.

Tree of Heaven

Ailanthus altissima

Make blue shadows on me,
small kings of shade.

I am flora and fauna,
orange groves and gold mines.

How to make their industry hum.
How to grow and wash their lemons.
I know.

They make dogs of us with bells,
with confused religion.

Their ravenous republic
swings us from tall buildings.

Our dead fold and fold,
sharper than needles.

My job is to dig, plant every town.
Of the years, say silence.

In this desert I need you, tree.
Grow into their weather

so that I can swell.
My spirit brims with seeds.

Say delta, ocean, sludge.
Say gold, mud,

say tracks, mountains,
say every little handmade brick.

Say rustle. Say breeze of thousands.

Marker of here—
in the dark of heaven.

Martian Chronicles

The wind-swept trees, you said, we left without thinking.
Back on solid earth.

>Small seeds stick in our shoes, trying
>to grow into every future possible.
>
>Still unplanted in our new sphere of rust.
>Is it Leopold's ghost we divine in the craters,
>
>pulling his plough through bone heaps? Reap
>a calcium feast, intestines filled with final teeth.

Carnivorous landscape, you said, not for our taking,
the way we ate the last world.

>The bridge we crossed is lined with dust.
>Even our dreams can't go back.
>
>Their pale ships sail the garnet plains
>and we aim our greatest hopes at them.

        The small kernels we sow become
        weapons, every sprout a shot fired.

Listen to each crackle, you said, in that lonely mixtape
you have on repeat.

        Crumbs in the labyrinth : a phantom finger pausing
        everything : an excess of empty between songs.

        This maroon sky is forever. It squeezes out
        new days like boulders, no birds to call them in.

        All we discover here already has a name, a place
        in an existing conversation, a ritual use.

We thought we knew, you said, what being human was.
It means nothing now.

Nanji no tame / for You

1.

Aliens to the ritual of bread.
Land fall. Fallen land. Leaven and arise.
Yeast, the great baker has landed.

2.

He who rises, attracts hammers.
Jesus is an illegal trailing croutons.
Brass horn, which wall to crumble?

Ten ni orareru watashi-tachi no Chichi yo
Minna ga sei to saremasu yōni
Mi kuni ga kimasu yo ni
Mi kokoro ga ten ni okona wareru tori
chi ni mo okonawaremasu yo uni
Watashitachi no hi goto no kate o kyo mo oatae kudasai

3.

Let us implant words. Tofu is no holy
metaphor. Soy does not a eucharist make.
What is your word for duty?

Brass horn, which wall to crumble?

4.

First pan on a vertiginous shore.
New true liturgy replaces amaterasu.
Native, someone died for you.

His body. Eat him and you
are protected by holy enterprise.
Iesu, sweet an-pan and advance scout.

Brass horn, which wall to crumble?

Nanji no tame ni atae tamaishi shu iesu kirisuto no karada
Nanji no tame ni nagashi tamaishi shu iesu kirisuto no chi
Pan sukika? Obāchan pan suki. Choco pan. Tabete.

You are now a people, you are filled.
Compulsion is freedom.
Is love. Open your ports. Rise. Eat.

汝のため／フォー・ユー

1.

異邦人がパンの祈りのために。
陸地発見。堕落した土地。発酵してふくらむ。
酵母。偉大なパン作りは上陸した。

2.

彼は起ち、金槌をひきつける。
主イエスは非合法に、パンくずを撒きながら進む。
金のラッパよ、どの城壁を落とすのか？

テンニ　オラレル　ワタシタチノ　チチヨ
ミナ　ガ　セイト　サレマス　ヨウニ
ミクニガ　キマス　ヨウニ
ミココロガ　テンニ　オコナワレル　トオリ
チニモ　オコナワレマス　ヨウニ
ワタシタチノ　ヒゴトノ　カテヲ　キョウモ　オアタエ　クダサイ

3.

単語を移植してみよう。トーフは聖なる
メタファーじゃない。大豆は聖餐の材料じゃない。
オツトメって何て訳すの?

金のラッパよ、どの城壁を落とすのか?

4.

はじめてのパーンが荒れた海の前に。
新たなる真の典礼がアマテラスを置き換える。
原住民よ、その方はあなたがたのために死なれたのだ。

彼の肉体。それを食べればあなたがたは
聖なる行ないによって守られるのです。
主イエス、甘い餡パーン、先乗りスカウト。

金のラッパよ、どの城壁を落とすのか?

ナンジノ　タメニ　アタエ　タマイシ　シュ　イエスキリストノ　カラダ
ナンジノ　タメニ　ナガシ　タマイシ　シュ　イエスキリストノ　チ
パーン、スキカー？　オバアチャン、パーン、スキー。チョコパーン。タベテ。

あなたがたは今や神のしもべとなり、満たされました。
強制こそが自由を生む。
それが愛だ。開港せよ。起て。食え。

田中庸介訳
Translation: Yosuke Tanaka

The Emperor Recognizes His Children

FIGURE 1. YI PO *(Father's Mother's Sisters)*

Perched on Tokyo red diner vinyl. Playing carefully
rehearsed people. Always rewriting the ship they rode from
Toufen, whipping the bow faster than seawater can close
behind. Swaying down the plank tongue, already Japanese.

Generation of Taichu-ken. Iron filings circling the
metropole, jettisoning their unwanted into the sea's darkest
maw. Nouveau mermaids, intimates of the red dawn.

FIGURE 2. QIA MEI PO *(Father's Sister's Husband's Mother)*

Bowing low for the chrysanthemum, etching herself into
its map. Warm embrace of childhood cartography. The
conductor announces Bioritsu, Shinchuku, and Taihoku,
hides Miaoli, Hsinchu, and Taipei in the bleed. Return
ticket to Tofun, not Toufen.

She remembers flowers, but not those laid at her
feet. Incense rides the humid morning up into
Hirohito's heaven.

Regal carriage of mind. Among her old, floated cities, the horse goes one way and she another. Oraga zaisho ni kite miyashanse. Recognize.

FIGURE 3. AH KUNG *(Father's Father)*

He fathers in two oceans, authorized by the Treaty of Shimonoseki. Begets a cigarette and sparkles. Comes back to Toufen with new clothes and new children. Expects rice in his old chipped bowl.

The horses look at him askance, want apples. The hens guard their eggs.

Three languages' worth of private thoughts pave his road to town. One to pay his taxes with and the other two for women. A sovereign island.

FIGURE 4. NGAI *(Father's Son)*

Born in Kyoto, on a fence, origin certified: Republic of
China, Ilha Formosa, Macross City, South Ataria. I am
camphor and electronics, a Tiger Balm spaceship.

In Toufen where only old-timers speak the
bureaucrats' archaic tongue. I am of, though
somehow not from. Ephemera.

I power up my battle mecha. Rotate mechanical waist,
crank head up. Flared sun in my giant black eyes. Whir,
grind, click. Years from any home.

My generations have each faced different flags, navigated
galaxies with dictionaries. We spacewalk, whisper into
each others' ears on the radio. Each of us a circling comet.

Ah Kung in the Philippine Jungle, 1945

Lush empty,
a map for battle.

In the blue undergrowth,
no wife, no songs, no daughters.

What part do you see first,
o conquering flora,

my step-republic, or my landscape
clothed in sky, not mine?

You undress me by the light
of rifle, sweat, radio.

My bare flag unfolds for you.
Your victory, a terrible beautiful.

My skin, not chrysanthemum.
But orchid cuffs, broken toe of moss.

Between conquerors,
how beautiful the clothed are.

But I am thumb, heel, tendon.
I am fauna.

Golden

for Hattori Yoshihiro

Ruffled chest wrapped
in disco gold, in pyrite chains
and tuxedo boogie. *Ah, ha, ha, ha.*
Painted with the fever of burning
lights, *wings of heaven on your shoes.*

The republic of meat hosts
this Saturday dance. Wants to
embroider notes in your frame,
wants to pluck the tendons
and tender fibers of you.

Reversal of numbers.
Your suspicious protein splayed
to the butcher's eye, how strange
its fibrous pieces, dangling scraps
before him. *Ah, ha, ha, ha.*

And how unpalatable your meat
to his homeowner's heart.
Feel the city breaking, his revolver
tattooing, tarnishing the night.
Ah, ha, ha, ha.
Ah, ha, ha, ha.

So that you are always sir, dear sir

for the Ayotzinapa 43 and all disappeared

I.

Ask me again why I am here
with this pine, this wild oyamel,
their great succulence of reason

You, machine lyric
and State, every state,
maker of rules and so outside them

You, hard blue evenings
with mass emergencies buried
inside them, like me

Your answers endlessly insufficient—
the mayor and his wife, smiling,
waving pinkies, waving dollar bills

Sweet water pouring
into the mind of a cardboard box
The verification of empty

II.

Dear sir, the angle of civilization
the angle of your civilization is too steep

I am speaking certain words and not others
Light rises along my spine

This mountain is a white bone
This republic, a one-note instrument

The president—like a president—deciding
is this one as human?

A forest of marigolds between our knees
"Mexicanos, ¿Cuándo piensas arder?
¿Cuando el desaparecido salga de tu casa?"

Our altars coated with sugar
no place outside the economy of war

When the pan is all gone we will take leave
a parade of ripples with a snake's purpose

This last remittance will cover the cost
if not I will send more, tied to an eagle

The earth is filled with exceptions—
43, a number, so many numbers

I feel around my dark hold
in search of light switch and decomposition

"Ayotzinapa vive
el estado ha muerto"

Bring back the fire

In the bow of our ship, an entrance
a bullet

Para que siempre sea el señor, estimado señor

para lxs 43 normalistas de Ayotzinapa y todxs lxs desaparecidxs

I.

Pregúntame otra vez qué estoy haciendo aquí
con este pino, este oyamel salvaje,
gran suculencia de razón la suya

Tú, lírica máquina
y el Estado, todo estado,
hacedor de reglas y tan inmune de ellas

Tú, duros atardeceres azules
con urgencias masivas enterradas
dentro de ellos, igual que yo

Tus respuestas incompletas sin fin—
El alcalde y su mujer, sonriendo,
blanden sus meñiques, blanden sus billetes

Agua dulce que diluvia
la mente de una caja de cartón
La verificación del vacío

II.

Apreciado señor, el ángulo de la civilización
el ángulo de su civilizacíon es demasiado escarpado

Digo ciertas palabras, y otras no
Una luz se levanta y recorre mi columna

Esta montaña es hueso blanco
Esta república, instrumento de una nota sola

El Presidente—como presidente—decide
¿es éste igual de humano?

Entre nuestras rodillas hay un bosque de cempasúchil
«Mexicanos, ¿cuándo piensas arder?
¿Cuando el desaparecido salga de tu casa?»

Nuestros altares garapiñados
No hay lugar fuera de la economía de guerra

Cuando el pan escasée, nos iremos
un desfile de ondulaciones con propósito de serpiente

Esta última remesa cubrirá lo que cuesta
si no, enviaré más, amarrado a una águila

La tierra, llena de excepciones—
43, un número, tantos números

Palpo en mi oscuro compartimiento
un interruptor de luz y podredumbre

«Ayotzinapa vive
el estado ha muerto»

Devuelvan el fuego

En la proa de nuestra nave, un acceso
Una bala

Traducción: Diego Flores Magón y Jen Hofer

Deconstruction: Capital

found poem

> LETTER FROM NADIA TOLOKONNIKOVA
> TO SLAVOJ ŽIŽEK

Dear Slavoj,

Two years of prison gave us sharp ears
    found in an endless search,
        inflamed according to the measure.

For our mission is to question
according to the economics of the gift.
    Provocative events

        sound the note A.
            This is the eternal world breath,
        the purpose of which is criticism.

In the autumn
this world has been
    and will eternally be living.

Not recognising any authority
in the pre-trial prison in Moscow,
the kingdom of absolute truth.

The rhythm of fire,
do not expect that it will be painless.

I could cut these experts down to size
sailing in a barrel.
We are a part of this force.

I visited you
in a dream, of course,
that has no absolute truths.

These elements are so connected,
dying away according to the measure.
There will always come a miracle.

Believe in the triumph of truth.
I see your argument about horses.
We are the children of Dionysus

and transformation.
Everyone else is used to hearing G flat.
We are the rebels asking for the storm

of mutual assistance.

Nadia

Memoriam for Places

May all devas be happy—
devas of sand and mud, of mold and dust.
devas of graveyards, of chalk lines
in the street, of bruises, and bullet holes.

May all devas without exception be at ease—
devas of bone, devas who sigh salt
in prison cell corners, in broken camps,
in red gallows, waterboards, and open ditches.

May I be mineral memoirist: ceremonial
witness: displeasure economist: ice thaw
eulogist: illecebrous operative.

All devas of neglected treaties in all
directions, of superfund sites, of oil spills,
and radioactive brown fields, devas
whose righteousness exceeds petition:

May all your stained places remember
how after rains, grass gets free.

Landing

1.

In a Manhattan church basement, my parents practice English.
Heads bent over thin workbooks, aura of old wood
and painted cement circling their crowns. He's watching
    fluorescence flit from the new steel bands on their fingers.

Together, they utter the holy words—*my name is, where is,
cream and sugar, please, thank you, when do you want it?*
The old nuns are kind, though they waved little flags
    at the victory parade.

By now nobody has to explain the three-in-one god. Japan dwells
in Taiwan, the US dwells in Japan, eternally. Now they cohabitate
in the stock market. Baptism by firebombs, atomics, Gojira.
    Hallowed course of study, this Manhattan project.

My English name is...

2.

Two labels, FROM: *something something* Japan, and TO: Us.
Cardboard box tightly fixed with brown tape and twine.
Just delivered, like me. Packed with Kyoto since too much
   New Jersey isn't good for our dreams.

It spills all over the clean linoleum, gutted. Brick muscles
of yokan, strung together with nori packets. Digestive
powders and a black heart of congealed herbs
   exhaling menthol slivers and dry orange peel dust.

Four liters of shoyu is better than a blood transfusion.
Probably the only cache in this echoing suburb
dotted with an epidemic of personal space.
   Package disemboweled, my parents read decades in the entrails.

   We empty the cupboards slowly.

Oboetaro / oboenakatta daro

answering machine greeting

hai, uwi aɾu ɴatu aɸeiɾaburu tsu teiku iyo kaɾu. pɾizu ɾivu iyoɾu ɴeim ændu ɴambaɾ. uwiɾu getu ba:ku tsu iyu asu suɴ asu posɪburu.

Deconstruction: Pink

your last hours are
deep fallen rose and
        broken pomegranate seeds
on hospital sheets
        still   body   warm
              you   might   return

        you do not need
anymore
    the pillow
        your cradle
    lost

    on the bathroom
    floor i
        hover

                                        dive
    for your
        hairs
                      extinct

                                    fruit.

Migratory Daughter

You've recycled your life,
        quit this ragged field
                leaving papers and
                        bones of language.
Undocumented
        bodhisattva,
                penumbra scattered
                        around us.
Citizen ship unswayed
        by the thirsty republic,
                no postal address
                        for the waxing moon.
Your letters bear kanji
        neat in /na ni nu ne/
                so no dreams
                        in English ka?
All your choices
        have followed you
                into the next.
                        So will mine.
Everyone is broken.
        Band-aids. Cedar and sage,

                  hot apple cider,
                            sharp rush of Tiger Balm.
People hurry forward
        as if unanimous,
                part the incoming tide
                        with oiled noses.
Forget dust. We are mostly water
        and so is the Earth.
                Ashes to ashes.
                        Water to generous water.

Heart Sutra After Cremation

Slice this any way you want. Mandolin
wisdom. Understand—no eyes, no teeth.
No bone chill, no fallen hair. No need
for liquid protein. O Shariputra, witness the
Pacific expanse smash on tender
shore. Tattoo compassion under my skin,
signal your radio, a spear from the future.

Clouds bend away without significance.
Translucent air mail, folded by my mother's hand.
      Rice paper tether, broken.

Write the sutra so neatly a bird reads it
from space, so tenderly my dead touches
her own cheek, startled.

Native Language

out there is gone to, pon!
riding a cup, goes up the river,
jiiiito looking, very dreamer boy is.

うん, fragments remembering does,
when speaking, inward bones lean do.
cho-important is, these mono.

why these mono recall happen doesn't?
sounds away slide, nyoro nyoro-like:
matta miru, miso shiru.

gutto! thinking does but itai itai comes
so sometimes forgetting better is, うん or
boat in, roretsu roretsu roretsu,

stream ni yukuri down float,
waku waku waku ureshii ni
life wa dream desu, ne. うん.

Letter to Myself II

after Adam Zagajewski

Go homeward with a suitcase full
of dew, gazing back
at red dawn just beginning.

Three tiny steps
to your train, but then a gulf so widened
a shinkansen swims for days.

Home is on no map, and explorers
will never find it. That time has passed.

Nor will any magic
return home to you, even the river
running toward it or the torii
framing its general magnificence.

Still, you remember
diesel-perfumed lawns emptied
cicada skins shrill
mosquito screen nights;

wet asphalt winds heavy
fumblings with girls steamy
purpled evenings
        starred and orchestrated by fireflies;

fiery mounds of leafy sweet decay;
mom's creased hands writing
        dark snowflakes of kanji;
echo of you and ah kung on a motorcycle;

green, alien fruits
of childhood, jerry-rigged
with simple explanations, injured
by routine.

Going may compel
many comforts, but also vague
dissatisfaction, this geography
without you in it.

No horse, taxi, or ship will
take you, and even if they do

no old friend or hotel will house you
because your residence papers are
from an old regime;

others have come to
take up your former life, and
all around, a barbarian country

so familiar, yet selling nothing
but the loss you have owned
        for years.

May These Words Be Worth Speech

All prayer comes from concrete,
sunflower butter and black tea,
caffeine to cross the distance.

Maybe a starfish sails the sky,
one arm doused in descent,
salt trickling from its mouth:
Come, come, come—nuclear bomb.

Children crouching with sand pails
at the ocean's curled and uncaring lip.
Unhorsed summer exits like a spy.
Beware the time of bright peace.

On the monied hill, a wine glass,
tense before the surgery of autumn.
Crash time is here.
It wants itself.

Long arc of my seasons.
Lean forward with palms up
and a god spills out.

Kneel in prayer.
Slip to the earth again and again.

How to Be an Orange

after Jeet Thayil

With sweetness
wave the flag of the republic.

Let bird henchmen go forth
when you're reduced
to juices.

Wander unremarkable towns
of wasted trucks and cacti
                heir to the nutritious earth.

                Unzip your sweet blood.
                The world machine doesn't care.

This land of dead ends and wax skin
        has a single mosquito for your eye.

        It's a hit or miss place.

You've been made bare
a country for others.

Your navel
on their tongues.

At least your cloud of history negates
their swollen ideas

                      about you.

Ease back and sigh a bee out onto your tongue.
      Purr an anthem

                that lodges
                in their backs.

Invite the flower you unfolded from
the birds that gave up their feathers
and the gasoline bitters.

On rain day
unfasten the cover of
your singular foliage—

show the ripe wrinkles
swollen around

summer incisions.

Taste your own
luscious

fissures.

Between the Two

When my father calls to say, you're not young anymore,
   I look at the wide sidewalk, the skyscrapers above me
      spilling dusk's lavender light.

Los Angeles' central library rears up, unzipping a hidden
   escarpment that tumbles into parking garage.
      It's true, the face of this city wasn't made for me, but

I've become the citizen of another country recently.
   Nobody looks at me the same way, I smell like someone else.
      My flank swells with the soft bites of their wishes.

Two faces. One for love and another for the DMV.
   Praise for dual-purpose artifacts—phone booths, popsicle sticks,
      hand shadows.

A monster pick-up straddles two parking spots
   and makes absurd claims—Army of One; Made in the USA.
      I'm thirsty for what can't be summarized.

Philosophers argue. Why he looks into the open face
   of Flower Street at that moment. Why he only calls his father
      on busy weekends, inside the vapor of sunset.

Dialectic of foxes and war medals. In the back
   and forth, green tea bitter from lingering too long, like me.
      I say to my father, don't claim me yet.

My new passport a test of my country's
   fidelity. It has nothing of mine I don't already
      know. The sultry evening, full of darkly thrown salt.

Deconstruction: Body Unbound

I.

This is how we get caught
in ghost architecture
intimate words of power

> *—extract from bodies the maximum time and force*

Machine hum
the richest years

Carceral bone-binding

> *—tactics of distribution,*
> *reciprocal adjustment of bodies,*
> *gestures and rhythms,*
> *differentiation of capacities,*
> *reciprocal coordination*

Elbows taut
at self-corrected angle

Precise
protein arrangement
    and spark distribution

Timetable of sinews
    and cartilage

We produce
through the useful gesture

        —hierarchical surveillance,
        continuous registration,
        perpetual assessment and classification

Technique of I
becoming a better I

Is this the efficiency
we sublimate for

Is this
the human

II.

Refuse to twist
Refuse to extract

> *—form is inconstant, feeling is inconstant,*
> *consciousness is inconstant*

Beyond legibility grows
the anti-republic

    undisciplined

> *—the stilling of all fabrications,*
> *the relinquishment of all acquisitions*

Burn all moxa
and reflect thus

Once were the uncared years
when imagination was schemata

Now
    unhinge
    the predictable I

Forward
the trembling labor of

    we

Notes

"Deconstruction: Papers" takes its punctuation cues from p. 1 of Theresa Hak Kyung Cha's *Dictee*.

"Powering Up" uses a line from Suzuki Roshi's *Zen Mind, Beginner's Mind* ("Just a swinging door") and refers to a basic computer programming language exercise to generate the phrase "Hello, world."

"The Ocean Swallows" references scenes from the 1968 film *Planet of the Apes*.

"Photo: Peach Boy in Kyoto" uses a phrase from Modern English's song "I Melt With You."

"Hakkas, the—" consists of index entries from *Japan and Her Colonies, Being Extracts From a Diary Made Whilst Visiting Formosa, Manchuria, Shantung, Korea and Saghalin in the Year 1921*, by Poultney Bigelow (1923).

"Deconstruction: No Government Can Hold a Hermit Crab" is after Charwei Tsai's "Day 4 - Hermit Crab," performance with hermit crabs, bricks, and black ink.

"My Dear Koxinga": Koxinga was a Ming Dynasty general born in Japan to a Chinese father and Japanese mother. After resisting the Manchu conquest, he eventually expelled the Dutch from Taiwan and ruled the island until his death. He is considered a hero by China, Taiwan, and Japan, but for different nationalist reasons.

"A Son Writes Back" responds to a 13th century qilu (eight lines, seven characters each) written by my ancestor and passed down in the family. Translated into English with my father. English stanzas follow eight line, seven syllable per line form.

"Migration: Like Paul Atreides" references David Lynch's movie *Dune*, based on Frank Herbert's science fiction book.

"Man Poem" contains lines from *Discipline and Punish* by Michel Foucault.

"His Pronouns Twitch" uses lines from Judith Butler's *Bodies That Matter* and a phrase from book 12, chapter 11 of the *Analects* (500 BCE) by Confucius: *Duke Ching of Chi asked Confucius about government. Confucius replied, "Let the ruler be a ruler, minister be a minister, father be a father, son be a son." The Duke said, "Excellent!*

Indeed, if the ruler is not a ruler, the ministers not ministers, fathers not fathers and sons not sons, even if I have food, how can I eat it?" Also contains lines from the I Ching (hexagram 36) in response to the question, "what is the best way to destroy patriarchy?"

"Tree of Heaven (Ailanthus altissima)" is a species of tree originally brought from East Asia. On the US West Coast, Chinese immigrants often planted Tree of Heaven where they settled because of its medicinal properties and the fact that it is a fast-growing shade-provider. It is usually considered by others to be an invasive nuisance.

"Nanji no tame / for You" uses Roman Catholic liturgy—The Lord's Prayer—in romanized Japanese.

"The Emperor Recognizes His Children" responds to generational effects of the Japanese colonial policy of kominka: "Given the imperial nation's mission, the position of Taiwan, and current world affairs, the imminent task is to have the five million islanders unite equally in acquiring the qualification of Japanese people, in reviewing their resolution together for the prosperity of the nation. In order to do so, we must strive for an extensive and thorough imperial spirit by promoting common education, rectifying proper language and customs, and cultivating the groundwork for loyal imperial subjects" (Kobayashi Seizo, Governor-General of Taiwan, 1937). Also referenced is a 1985 television anime series, *Robotech*, which was based on a Japanese anime series.

"Golden" is for Hattori Yoshihiro, a Japanese exchange student living in Baton Rouge, Louisiana. On October 17, 1992, Yoshihiro and his homestay classmate went to a Halloween party. Yoshihiro was dressed as John Travolta from *Saturday Night Fever*. The two went to the wrong address and the homeowner, Rodney Peairs, shot Yoshihiro at point blank range, killing him. Peairs was acquitted after a seven-day trial and three and a quarter hours of jury deliberation. The poem uses lyrics from the Bee-Gees', "Stayin' Alive."

"Deconstruction: Capital" is composed entirely of words found in a published letter between Russian Pussy Riot band leader Nadia Tolokonnikova and Slovenian philosopher Slavoj Žižek while Tolokonnikova was in prison in 2013.

"Memoriam for Places" is based on a Theravadan Buddhist lovingkindness prayer.

"Oboetaro / oboenakatta daro" uses the International Phonetic Alphabet to try to reconstruct my mother's voice from memory. Oboetaro is the past presumptive conjugation of oboe, the Japanese word for "remember." Oboenakatta daro is the negative past presumptive conjugation. To presume to remember leaves some room for doubt.

"Heart Sutra after Cremation" is after Charwei Tsai's "Tofu Mantra II," black ink on fresh tofu. It uses patterns ("no…") and phrases ("Oh Shariputra") from the Mahayana Buddhist Heart Sutra.

"Native Language" uses Japanese onomatopoeia and ideophones in combination with Japanese American vernacular.

"May These Words Be Worth Speech" uses a line from Morrissey's, "Everyday is Like Sunday."

"Deconstruction: Body" uses lines from *Discipline and Punish* by Michel Foucault and the Theravadan Buddhist Girimananda Sutta.

Gratitude 合掌

The learning needed to create this poetry collection came through the input of many people who are themselves incredible writers. Deep thanks first and foremost to Vickie Vértiz, an amazing writer and artist who has supported the development of this book at all stages. To Hari Alluri, Xochitl-Julisa Bermejo, Rachelle Cruz, Mia Ayumi Malhotra, Barbara Jane Reyes, and Margaret Rhee for reading and giving invaluable feedback. To VONA/Voices and Suheir Hammad, who told me I was ready. To Finishing Line Press, which published my first chapbook at just the right time.

Thank you also to: Patricia Ikeda, dharma friend and poet, for long-believing in my writing. Angana Chatterji and Richard Shapiro, for embodying the joy of decolonial thought. *Kartika Review*, through which I gained a wider education in emerging Asian Pacific American poetry. Sunny Woan, for lawyerly and spiritual advice. Jen Hofer, Suh-Ling Lin, Yuh-Lang Liu, Diego Flores Magón, Yosuke Tanaka, Vickie Vértiz, and Der-Jin Woan for translations.

To many others, including Neelanjana Banerjee, Don Mee Choi, Sesshu Foster, Bhanu Kapil, Lisa Marie Rollins, Brandon Shimoda, Mike Sonksen, Aimee Suzara, Bryan Thao Worra, and everyone in The Grind for support in a variety of ways. To the Djerassi Resident Artist Program, Community of Writers, Kundiman, and VONA/Voices for the community, space, and time to just write. Thank you.

To Chad Sweeney, Cati Porter, and Inlandia Institute, thank you for believing in this book.

Acknowlegements

A number of poems in this book were previously published in the following places, in various states of change:

LITERARY JOURNALS
Action, Yes!, "汝のため/フォー・ユー"; *Asian American Literary Journal*, "Landing"; *The Baltimore Review*, "Heart Sutra after Cremation"; *Barrow Street*, "Between the Two" and "Your Father Tongue"; *Codex*, "Golden"; *The Collagist*, "Ah Kung in the Philippine Jungle, 1945"; *CURA*, "Martian Chronicles"; *Eye to the Telescope*, "Migration: Like Paul Atreides"; *Generations*, "Overdue Notices," "In Orbit Around New York City," and "Immigration: Slide 78"; *La casa del hijo de el Ahuizote*, "Para que siempre sea señor, estimado señor"; *Kartika Review*, "Being Born is Also a Ghost"; *Lantern Review*, "A Son Writes Back"; *Los Angeles Review*, "Tree of Heaven"; *Ozone Park Journal*, "Nanji no tame / for You" and "Memoriam"; *The Pinch*, "Migratory Daughter" and "Deconstruction: Capital"; *RHINO*, "A History of My Complexion"; *The Rumpus*, "Deconstruction: Citizenship"; Split This Rock's Poem of the Week, "Elegy for Kimani Gray" and "So that you are always sir, dear sir"; *TAYO*, "Deconstruction: Body Unbound" and "Man Poem"; *Vinyl*, "Search History"

ANTHOLOGIES
Dismantle, "Native Language"; *Orangelandia*, "How to be an Orange"

CHAPBOOKS
You Left Without Your Shoes, "Deconstruction: Pink"

Photo credit: Margarita Corporan

Kenji C. Liu's writing appears in *The American Poetry Review*, *Action Yes!*, *Asian American Literary Review*, *Barrow Street Journal*, *CURA*, Split This Rock's poem of the week series, several anthologies, and many other places. He is also author of the poetry chapbook *You Left Without Your Shoes*. A recipient of fellowships from Kundiman, VONA/Voices, Djerassi Resident Artist Program, and Community of Writers, he holds an MA in Cultural Anthropology and Social Transformation.

CPSIA information can be obtained at www.ICGtesting.com
Printed in the USA
BVOW02s1129100316

439669BV00002B/3/P